MASTERING THE ART OF
CLOSING DEALS

STEP BY STEP GUIDE ON HOW TO CLOSE DEALS

JOSEPHINE ANDERSON

Copyright © 2024 by Josephine Anderson

Protected by copyright law. No piece of this distribution might be imitated, put away or communicated in any structure or using any and all means, electronic, mechanical, copying, recording, examining, or in any case without composed authorization from the distributor.
It is against the law to duplicate this book, present it on a site, or circulate it by some other means without consent.
Josephine Anderson states the ethical right to be distinguished as the creator of this work.

Table of Content

Introduction

1. Understanding Your Prospect
   - Researching Your Audience
   - Identifying Pain Points and Needs

2. Building Relationships
   - Establishing Trust and Credibility
   - Effective Communication Strategies

3. The Sales Process
   - Qualifying Leads
   - Presenting Solutions
   - Handling Objections

4. Advanced Closing Techniques
   - Creating a Sense of Urgency
   - Using Persuasive Language
   - Trial Closes and Assumptive Closes

5. Negotiation Strategies
   - Maximizing Value for Both Parties
   - Win-Win Negotiation Tactics

6. Overcoming Common Challenges
   - Dealing with Rejection

- Handling Difficult Clients

7. Closing the Deal
   - Asking for the Sale
   - Closing Techniques for Different Scenarios

8. Follow-Up and Customer Retention
   - Post-Sale Relationship Building
   - Ensuring Customer Satisfaction

9. Measuring Success
   - Key Performance Indicators
   - Analyzing and Improving Closing Rates

10. Case Studies and Examples
    - Real-Life Scenarios and Solutions

Conclusion

INTRODUCTION

In the dynamic landscape of business, success often hinges on one critical skill: the ability to close deals. Whether you're an entrepreneur, a sales professional, or an aspiring business leader, mastering the art of negotiation and sales is essential for achieving your goals and driving growth. In "Closing Deals," we look deep into the strategies, tactics, and mindset required to excel in the competitive arena of deal-making.

Closing deals isn't just about sealing transactions; it's about creating value, forging relationships, and driving mutual benefit. Every successful deal represents a culmination of effort, strategy, and communication. It's the moment when all the pieces come together, and opportunities transform into tangible results. From securing lucrative contracts to building long-term partnerships, the art of closing deals is the cornerstone of business success.

At its core, closing deals is about selling - not just products or services, but ideas, solutions, and opportunities. Whether you're pitching to a potential client or persuading stakeholders to buy into your vision, the sales process is a multifaceted journey that requires skillful execution at every stage. From prospecting and qualifying leads to delivering compelling presentations and overcoming objections, we dissect each phase of the sales cycle, equipping you with the tools and techniques needed to close deals effectively.

Success in closing deals isn't just about what you do; it's also about how you think. A winning mindset is essential for overcoming challenges, staying resilient in the face of rejection, and maintaining focus amidst distractions. In this book, we explore the habits, attitudes, and beliefs that separate top performers from the rest. By cultivating a mindset of abundance, adaptability, and relentless pursuit of excellence, you can unlock your full potential and achieve extraordinary results in your deal-making endeavors.

Each chapter offers valuable insights, practical strategies, and real-world examples to help you sharpen your skills and elevate your performance. Whether you're a novice looking to learn the ropes or a professional seeking to refine your approach, this book is your roadmap to success in the exhilarating world of negotiation and sales. So, buckle up, embrace the challenge, and prepare to conquer new horizons as you embark on the path to closing deals like never before.

1

Understanding your prospects

Researching Your Audience

Researching your audience is similar to embarking on a captivating expedition into the complex details of human behavior, motivations, and preferences. It's a multifaceted journey that transcends mere data collection, delving deep into the psyche of your target demographic to unveil insights that inform strategic decisions and foster meaningful connections. Let's embark on this immersive exploration of the art and science of researching your audience

1. **Understanding the Human Element**
At its core, audience research is about understanding people—their desires, fears, aspirations, and idiosyncrasies. It's about peering beyond superficial demographics to unravel the intricate layers of human behavior and psychology that shape their decisions. By embracing the human element, you gain empathy and insight into the minds and hearts of your audience, laying the groundwork for authentic engagement and connection.

2. **Demographic Insights**
Demographic data provides the foundational framework for understanding your audience. It encompasses variables such as age, gender, location, income, and education level, offering valuable insights into the composition of your target demographic. By analyzing demographic trends, you gain a broad understanding of who your audience is and where they reside, enabling you to tailor your messaging and strategies accordingly.

3. **Psychographic Profiling**
Beyond demographics lies the realm of psychographics—the attitudes, values, lifestyles, and aspirations that shape individuals' preferences and behaviors. Psychographic profiling delves deep into the psyche of your audience, uncovering their beliefs, interests, hobbies, and purchasing habits. By segmenting your audience based on psychographic variables, you gain a nuanced understanding of their motivations and desires, allowing you to craft highly targeted and resonant marketing campaigns.

4. **Behavioral Analysis**
Behavioral analysis focuses on how individuals interact with your brand across various touchpoints and channels. It involves tracking user engagement

metrics, such as website visits, email opens, social media interactions, and purchase history, to discern patterns and preferences. By understanding your audience's behaviors and preferences, you can optimize user experiences, personalize content, and deliver targeted messaging that resonates with their needs and interests.

5. **Market Research and Trend Analysis**
Keeping a finger on the pulse of market trends and industry developments is essential for staying ahead of the curve. Market research involves monitoring industry trends, competitor activities, and consumer insights to identify emerging opportunities and threats. By conducting market research and trend analysis, you gain valuable intelligence that informs product development, marketing strategies, and business decisions, ensuring your offerings remain relevant and competitive in a dynamic marketplace.

6. **Customer Feedback and Surveys**
Listening to the voice of your audience is paramount for gaining valuable insights and feedback. Customer feedback mechanisms, such as surveys, interviews, and focus groups, provide direct channels for soliciting input and understanding customer perceptions. By actively soliciting and analyzing customer feedback, you gain actionable insights that drive product

innovation, service improvements, and customer satisfaction initiatives, fostering loyalty and advocacy.

7. **Data Analytics and Insights**
In today's data-driven landscape, leveraging analytics and insights is critical for deriving actionable intelligence from vast datasets. Data analytics tools enable you to analyze user behavior, track key performance indicators, and derive actionable insights that inform decision-making. By harnessing the power of data analytics, you can identify trends, optimize marketing campaigns, and measure the impact of your efforts, driving continuous improvement and growth.

8. **Iterative Learning and Optimization**
Audience research is not a one-time activity but an ongoing process of iterative learning and optimization. It involves continuously gathering feedback, testing hypotheses, and refining strategies based on real-time insights and feedback. By embracing a culture of experimentation and iteration, you remain agile and responsive to changing market dynamics, ensuring your strategies remain relevant and effective over time.

In essence, researching your audience is a dynamic and multifaceted endeavor that blends art and science to unravel the mysteries of human behavior and preferences. By embracing empathy, curiosity, and data-driven insights, you can gain a deep understanding of your audience, forge authentic connections, and drive meaningful engagement that transcends transactional interactions.

Identifying Pain Points and Needs

Exploring the profound realm of identifying pain points and needs unveils a transformative journey of empathy, insight, and innovation. It's similar to embarking on an expedition into the depths of human experience, where every discovery illuminates a path towards delivering meaningful solutions and fostering lasting connections. Let's immerse ourselves in the vast expanse of this critical aspect of understanding your audience

1. Empathy as the Compass

Identifying pain points and needs begins with empathy—the ability to step into the shoes of your audience and truly understand their challenges, frustrations, and aspirations. It's about listening with an open heart and mind, seeking to understand the world through their eyes. By cultivating empathy, you can develop a deep sense of connection with your audience, laying the groundwork for meaningful engagement and lasting relationships.

2. **Unveiling the Layers of Complexity**
Pain points and needs are like layers of an onion, each one revealing a deeper dimension of the human experience. They can manifest in various forms, from practical challenges and obstacles to emotional struggles and desires. Identifying pain points requires peeling back these layers, delving beyond surface-level observations to uncover the underlying motivations and aspirations that drive behavior.

3. **Listening with Intention**
Active listening is the cornerstone of identifying pain points and needs. It involves more than just hearing words—it's about listening with intention, empathy, and curiosity. Paying close attention to verbal cues, body language, and emotional nuances enables you to discern the subtle signals that hint at unmet needs and unresolved pain points. By listening attentively, you demonstrate respect, empathy, and a genuine desire to understand your audience's perspective.

4. **Asking the Right Questions**
Effective questioning is a powerful tool for uncovering pain points and needs. By asking probing questions that encourage reflection and introspection, you can elicit valuable insights into your audience's challenges, desires, and aspirations. Open-ended questions, such as "What are your biggest challenges?" or "What

would make your life easier?" invite deeper exploration and encourage honest, candid responses.

5. Mining Insights from Data

Data analysis provides a treasure trove of insights into your audience's behavior and preferences. By analyzing quantitative data, such as website analytics, sales trends, and customer feedback, you can identify patterns, trends, and correlations that reveal underlying pain points and needs. Qualitative data, such as customer surveys, interviews, and social media interactions, offers rich, nuanced insights into the emotional and experiential dimensions of your audience's journey.

6. Mapping the Customer Journey

Pain points and needs are not static—they evolve and shift over the course of the customer journey. Mapping the customer journey enables you to pinpoint the moments of friction, frustration, and delight that shape your audience's experience. By understanding the touchpoints where pain points arise and needs emerge, you can tailor your marketing strategies and offerings to address them proactively, fostering a seamless, frictionless customer experience.

7. **Identifying Unmet Needs and Opportunities**
Pain points and needs are not always obvious—they often lurk beneath the surface, waiting to be discovered. By conducting thorough research and analysis, you can uncover unmet needs and hidden opportunities that your audience may not even be aware of. These unexplored territories represent fertile ground for innovation and differentiation, enabling you to create solutions that resonate deeply with your audience and set you apart from competitors.

8. **Iterative Refinement and Innovation**
Identifying pain points and needs is not a one-time exercise—it's an ongoing process of iterative refinement and innovation. By continuously gathering feedback, analyzing data, and adapting your strategies, you can stay attuned to evolving customer needs and market dynamics. This iterative approach empowers you to refine your offerings, enhance your value proposition, and deliver exceptional experiences that meet the ever-changing needs of your audience.

In essence, identifying pain points and needs is a transformative journey of empathy, insight, and innovation. By listening attentively, asking the right questions, and mining insights from data, you can uncover the hidden dimensions of your audience's experience, paving the way for meaningful connections and impactful solutions. Embrace this journey with an open heart and mind, and you'll unlock a world of possibilities for delivering value and fostering lasting relationships with your audience.

2

Building Relationships

Establishing Trust and Credibility

Exploring the profound terrain of establishing trust and credibility unveils a transformative journey of authenticity, integrity, and connection. It's similar to embarking on a quest to build bridges of confidence and reliability that span the chasm between brands and their audiences. Let's look into more details on the critical aspect of relationship-building

1. The Bedrock of Relationships
Trust and credibility serve as the bedrock upon which all meaningful relationships are built. They form the foundation of mutual understanding, respect, and loyalty that underpins successful interactions between brands and their audiences. Establishing trust is not just a goal—it's a fundamental imperative for fostering genuine connections and driving long-term engagement and loyalty.

2. Authenticity as a North Star
Authenticity is the cornerstone of trust and credibility. It's about being genuine, transparent, and true to your values and promises. Authentic brands don't just talk

the talk—they walk the walk, consistently delivering on their commitments and acting with integrity in every interaction. By embodying authenticity in their actions and communications, brands can forge deep, meaningful connections with their audiences based on mutual respect and trust.

3. **Consistency Builds Confidence**

Consistency breeds confidence. It's about delivering a consistent experience across every touchpoint and interaction, from your marketing messages to your customer service interactions. Consistent brands inspire trust because they're reliable—they do what they say they'll do, time and time again. By maintaining consistency in your actions and communications, you demonstrate reliability and dependability, fostering trust and credibility with your audience.

4. **Transparency Fosters Trust**

Transparency is the antidote to skepticism and doubt. It's about being open, honest, and forthcoming in your communications, even when the message is difficult or uncomfortable. Transparent brands don't hide behind smoke and mirrors—they're upfront about their practices, policies, and processes, and they're willing to admit when they make mistakes. By embracing transparency, brands can build trust by showing their audience that they have nothing to hide and that they're committed to honesty and integrity.

5. Empathy Builds Bridges

Empathy is the bridge that connects brands with their audiences on a human level. It's about understanding your audience's needs, concerns, and aspirations and showing genuine compassion and understanding. Empathetic brands don't just sell products or services—they solve problems and make people's lives better. By demonstrating empathy in your actions and communications, you can build trust by showing your audience that you care about their well-being and are committed to helping them achieve their goals.

6. Social Proof as Validation

Social proof is a powerful tool for building trust and credibility. It's about leveraging the experiences and opinions of others to validate your brand's claims and promises. Testimonials, reviews, and user-generated content provide tangible evidence of your brand's value and reliability, helping to alleviate doubts and build confidence in your offerings. By showcasing social proof, brands can build trust by demonstrating that they have a track record of delivering positive outcomes for their customers.

7. Expertise Commands Respect

Expertise is a cornerstone of credibility. It's about demonstrating knowledge, authority, and competence in your field, positioning your brand as a trusted source of information and guidance. Brands that showcase their expertise through thought leadership, educational content, and industry insights can build credibility by demonstrating their deep understanding of their audience's needs and challenges. By positioning yourself as an expert in your field, you can build trust by showing your audience that you have the knowledge and expertise to help them achieve their goals.

8. Delivering on Promises

Ultimately, trust and credibility are earned through action, not words. It's about delivering on your promises and consistently exceeding expectations in every interaction. Brands that consistently deliver value, quality, and exceptional experiences build trust by demonstrating that they can be relied upon to deliver results. By consistently delivering on your promises, you can build credibility by showing your audience that you're committed to their success and satisfaction.

Establishing trust and credibility is a transformative journey of authenticity, consistency, and empathy. By embodying authenticity, consistency, and transparency in your actions and communications, demonstrating empathy and understanding towards your audience's needs and concerns, and showcasing social proof and expertise, you can build deep, meaningful connections with your audience based on trust and credibility. Embrace this journey with sincerity and integrity, and you'll lay the foundation for enduring relationships and sustained success.

Effective Communication Strategies

Exploring the vast landscape of effective communication strategies unveils a dynamic journey of connection, persuasion, and influence. It's similar to navigating a rich tapestry of words, gestures, and emotions to convey messages that resonate deeply with your audience. Let's embark on an immersive exploration of this critical aspect of interpersonal and professional success

1. **The Power of Words**

Words have the power to inspire, inform, and ignite action. Effective communication begins with choosing the right words to convey your message clearly and concisely. It's about crafting compelling narratives that capture attention, evoke emotion, and drive engagement. By choosing your words thoughtfully and purposefully, you can create connections with your audience that endure long after the conversation ends.

2. Active Listening as a Foundation

Effective communication is a two-way street—it requires not only speaking but also listening with intention and empathy. Active listening involves fully engaging with the speaker, paying attention to their words, tone, and body language, and seeking to understand their perspective. By listening actively, you demonstrate respect, empathy, and a genuine interest in the other person's thoughts and feelings, fostering trust and understanding in the process.

3. Clarity and Conciseness

Clarity and conciseness are essential elements of effective communication. It's about conveying your message in a clear, straightforward manner that leaves no room for ambiguity or misunderstanding. Avoiding jargon, technical language, and unnecessary complexity ensures that your message resonates with your audience and can be easily understood by all. By prioritizing clarity and conciseness, you can cut through the noise and capture your audience's attention with precision and impact.

4. Tailoring Your Message

Effective communication is not one-size-fits-all—it's about tailoring your message to resonate with your audience's needs, interests, and preferences. This involves understanding your audience's demographics, psychographics, and communication styles and adapting your message accordingly. Whether you're addressing a diverse group or a specific individual, customizing your message ensures that it resonates with your audience on a personal level, driving engagement and fostering connection.

5. Emotional Intelligence in Action

Emotional intelligence plays a crucial role in effective communication. It's about understanding and managing your own emotions while also empathizing with the emotions of others. By recognizing and acknowledging the emotions underlying communication, you can respond with empathy and sensitivity, building trust and understanding with your audience. Emotional intelligence enables you to navigate difficult conversations with grace and diplomacy, fostering understanding and collaboration in even the most challenging situations.

6. Nonverbal Communication

Nonverbal communication—such as body language, facial expressions, and gestures—plays a significant role in conveying messages and building understanding. Paying attention to nonverbal cues enables you to gauge your audience's reactions and adjust your communication style accordingly. By aligning your nonverbal communication with your verbal message, you can enhance clarity, sincerity, and authenticity, fostering deeper connections with your audience.

7. Building Trust through Transparency

Trust is the foundation of effective communication. It's about being honest, transparent, and authentic in your interactions, even when the message is difficult or uncomfortable. By communicating openly and transparently, you demonstrate integrity and reliability, building trust and credibility with your audience. Transparency fosters open dialogue, collaboration, and mutual respect, laying the groundwork for meaningful and enduring relationships.

8. Feedback and Adaptation

Effective communication is a continuous process of feedback and adaptation. It's about soliciting input from your audience, listening to their feedback, and adjusting your message and approach accordingly. By seeking feedback and adapting to changing circumstances, you demonstrate responsiveness and flexibility, fostering engagement and collaboration with your audience. Continuous improvement ensures that your communication remains relevant, impactful, and resonant over time.

In essence, effective communication is a dynamic interplay of words, actions, and emotions aimed at fostering connection, understanding, and collaboration. By embracing active listening, clarity, empathy, and transparency, and tailoring your message to resonate with your audience's needs and preferences, you can build trust, drive engagement, and achieve meaningful outcomes in both personal and professional interactions. Embrace these strategies with sincerity and intention, and you'll unlock the power of effective communication to create lasting impact and positive change.

3

The Sales Process

Qualifying Leads

Qualifying leads is a pivotal aspect of the sales process, related to sifting through a treasure trove to uncover gems of opportunity. It involves discerning which prospects have the greatest potential for conversion, thereby maximizing the efficiency and effectiveness of your sales efforts. Let's carry out a comprehensive exploration on this important phase.

1. **Defining the Ideal Prospect**
Qualifying leads begins with a clear understanding of your ideal customer profile—the characteristics, traits, and attributes that signify a good fit for your product or service. This involves analyzing past successes, identifying commonalities among your most valuable customers, and creating a profile that serves as a blueprint for prospect qualification. By defining your ideal prospect, you can focus your efforts on engaging with leads who are most likely to convert, saving time and resources in the process.

2. **Understanding Needs and Pain Points**
Effective lead qualification requires a deep understanding of your prospect's needs, pain points, and aspirations. It's about asking probing questions, actively listening to their responses, and uncovering the underlying motivations driving their interest in your offering. By empathizing with your prospect's challenges and aspirations, you can tailor your messaging and solutions to address their specific needs, increasing the likelihood of conversion.

3. **Assessing Budget and Authority**
Two critical factors in lead qualification are budget and authority. Budget refers to the financial resources available to the prospect for purchasing your product or service, while authority pertains to their decision-making power within the organization. Qualifying leads involves assessing whether the prospect has the budget to afford your offering and the authority to make purchasing decisions. By identifying prospects who meet these criteria, you can prioritize your efforts on engaging with decision-makers who have the ability to move forward with the buying process.

4. **Evaluating Timeline and Urgency**
Timing is crucial in lead qualification. Understanding the prospect's timeline and sense of urgency can help

you prioritize leads and allocate resources effectively. Qualifying leads involves assessing whether the prospect has an immediate need for your product or service, or if their buying timeline is more long-term. By identifying prospects with a pressing need or timeline, you can focus your efforts on opportunities that are more likely to convert in the near future, while nurturing longer-term prospects over time.

5. **Aligning with Ideal Use Cases**

Not all leads are created equal, and qualifying leads involves assessing whether the prospect's use case aligns with the strengths and capabilities of your offering. It's about identifying prospects who stand to benefit the most from your product or service, based on their specific needs, challenges, and objectives. By aligning with ideal use cases, you can position your offering as the perfect solution to address the prospect's pain points, increasing the likelihood of conversion.

6. **Scoring and Prioritization**

Lead scoring is a valuable tool for prioritizing leads based on their likelihood to convert. It involves assigning numerical values to various lead attributes, such as demographic information, engagement level, and purchase intent, and using this data to rank leads in order of priority. By scoring and prioritizing leads, you can focus your attention on high-value opportunities that are most likely to result in sales, while deprioritizing leads with lower conversion potential.

7. Continuous Iteration and Improvement

Lead qualification is not a one-time event—it's an ongoing process of continuous iteration and improvement. It involves analyzing data, gathering feedback, and refining your qualification criteria based on real-world results. By constantly evaluating and optimizing your lead qualification process, you can adapt to changing market dynamics, refine your targeting strategies, and improve the efficiency and effectiveness of your sales efforts over time.

In essence, qualifying leads is a strategic endeavor that requires a combination of data analysis, empathy, and strategic thinking. By defining your ideal prospect, understanding their needs and pain points, assessing budget and authority, evaluating timeline and urgency, aligning with ideal use cases, and scoring and prioritizing leads, you can maximize the efficiency and effectiveness of your sales efforts, driving meaningful results and fostering long-term success.

Presenting Solutions

Presenting solutions is a dynamic and pivotal phase in the sales process, it's related to unveiling a masterful work of art that addresses the unique needs and challenges of your prospects. It's a nuanced dance of communication, persuasion, and problem-solving, where every word and gesture is carefully crafted to resonate with your audience and drive action. Let's embark on an immersive exploration of this critical aspect of salesmanship

1. **Understanding the Problem**
Effective solution presentation begins with a deep understanding of the prospect's needs, pain points, and aspirations. It's about listening attentively, asking probing questions, and empathizing with the challenges they face. By understanding the problem from the prospect's perspective, you can tailor your solution to address their specific needs and priorities, increasing the likelihood of a successful outcome.

2. **Customizing the Solution**
No two prospects are alike, and neither are their problems. Effective solution presentation involves customizing your offering to meet the unique needs

and preferences of each prospect. This may involve tailoring your product or service features, pricing, and terms to align with their specific requirements. By demonstrating flexibility and adaptability in your approach, you can show your prospect that you're committed to finding the right solution for their individual needs.

3. **Highlighting Value Proposition**

Your solution presentation is an opportunity to showcase the value proposition of your offering and differentiate yourself from the competition. It's about clearly articulating the benefits and advantages of your product or service and how it addresses the prospect's needs better than any alternative. By highlighting the unique value proposition of your offering, you can capture the prospect's attention and demonstrate why your solution is the best choice for their needs.

4. **Visualizing Success**

Effective solution presentation goes beyond words—it's about painting a vivid picture of the prospect's future success with your offering. This may involve using visual aids, such as charts, graphs, and case studies, to illustrate the potential benefits and outcomes of choosing your solution. By helping the prospect visualize the positive impact your offering can have on their business or life, you can inspire confidence and excitement about moving forward with the purchase.

5. Addressing Objections and Concerns

Solution presentation is also an opportunity to address any objections or concerns the prospect may have about your offering. This requires active listening and empathy to understand the root cause of their objections and respond with empathy and clarity. By addressing objections directly and providing reassurance and evidence to support your claims, you can alleviate doubts and build trust with the prospect.

6. Creating a Compelling Narrative

Every solution presentation is a story waiting to be told—a narrative that captures the prospect's imagination and compels them to take action. It's about framing your offering in a way that resonates with the prospect's values, goals, and aspirations, and guides them on a journey towards a positive outcome. By crafting a compelling narrative that speaks to the prospect's emotions and motivations, you can create a sense of urgency and excitement about choosing your solution.

7. Demonstrating Expertise and Authority

Solution presentation is an opportunity to showcase your expertise and authority in your field. It's about positioning yourself as a trusted advisor and thought leader who can guide the prospect towards success. By sharing insights, best practices, and success stories related to your offering, you can demonstrate your knowledge and credibility, building confidence and trust with the prospect.

8. Closing with Confidence

The final step in solution presentation is closing the deal with confidence and conviction. This requires asking for the sale directly and confidently, while also respecting the prospect's decision-making process. By expressing enthusiasm and confidence in your solution and emphasizing the benefits of moving forward, you can inspire the prospect to take action and commit to the purchase.

In essence, presenting solutions is an art and a science that requires a combination of empathy, creativity, and persuasion. By understanding the prospect's needs, customizing your solution, highlighting value proposition, visualizing success, addressing objections, creating a compelling narrative, demonstrating expertise, and closing with confidence, you can effectively guide prospects towards choosing your solution and achieving their goals. Embrace this process with passion and purpose, and you'll unlock the power of solution presentation to drive meaningful outcomes and foster long-term success.

Handling Objections

Handling objections is a fundamental skill in sales, it's related to navigating through obstacles to reach the treasure at the end of the journey. It's a delicate dance of empathy, persuasion, and problem-solving, where each objection presents an opportunity to deepen understanding and build trust with the prospect. Let's embark on a comprehensive exploration of this critical aspect of salesmanship

1. **Embracing Objections as Opportunities**

Objections are not roadblocks—they're signposts pointing the way to a deeper understanding of the prospect's needs and concerns. Effective objection handling begins with embracing objections as opportunities for engagement and learning. It's about approaching objections with curiosity and empathy, seeking to understand the underlying motivations and addressing them in a way that builds trust and understanding with the prospect.

2. **Active Listening and Empathy**
The foundation of effective objection handling lies in active listening and empathy. It's about tuning in to the prospect's concerns, validating their feelings, and demonstrating genuine understanding and compassion. By listening attentively and acknowledging the validity of the prospect's objections, you can create a supportive environment where open dialogue and mutual respect can flourish.

3. **Clarifying and Uncovering Root Causes**
Often, objections are symptoms of deeper underlying concerns or misunderstandings. Effective objection handling involves clarifying the prospect's objections and uncovering the root causes behind them. This may involve asking probing questions, digging deeper into the prospect's concerns, and uncovering any misconceptions or misinterpretations that may be driving their objections. By addressing the root causes of objections, you can alleviate doubts and build confidence in your offering.

4. **Responding with Value and Evidence**
Once you understand the prospect's objections, it's essential to respond with value and evidence that address their concerns directly. This may involve highlighting the benefits and advantages of your offering, providing case studies or testimonials that

demonstrate its effectiveness, or offering tangible evidence to support your claims. By responding with value and evidence, you can build credibility and confidence in your solution, overcoming objections and moving the conversation forward.

5. Turning Objections into Opportunities

Effective objection handling is about reframing objections as opportunities for collaboration and problem-solving. Instead of seeing objections as obstacles to be overcome, view them as invitations to engage in a constructive dialogue with the prospect. This may involve brainstorming alternative solutions, offering compromises or concessions, or exploring creative ways to address the prospect's concerns. By turning objections into opportunities, you can demonstrate your commitment to finding the best possible solution for the prospect's needs, building trust and understanding in the process.

6. Handling Objections Proactively

Anticipating and addressing objections before they arise is a proactive approach to objection handling. By understanding common objections that prospects may have and preparing responses in advance, you can be better equipped to address them effectively during the sales conversation. This may involve creating objection handling scripts, conducting role-playing exercises with your team, or gathering feedback from past interactions to identify recurring objections and develop strategies for addressing them proactively.

7. Seeking Win-Win Solutions

Effective objection handling is not about winning arguments—it's about finding win-win solutions that satisfy the needs and concerns of both parties. It's about approaching objections with a spirit of collaboration and mutual respect, seeking to find common ground and reach a positive outcome together. By demonstrating flexibility, creativity, and a willingness to compromise, you can build trust and goodwill with the prospect, fostering a positive and productive relationship that extends beyond the initial sale.

8. Following Up and Revisiting

Objection handling doesn't end with the initial conversation—it's an ongoing process of follow-up and revisiting. After addressing the prospect's objections, it's essential to follow up with additional information, reassurance, or clarification as needed. This demonstrates your commitment to addressing the prospect's concerns and provides an opportunity to reinforce the value proposition of your offering. By staying engaged and responsive throughout the objection handling process, you can build trust and confidence with the prospect and increase the likelihood of a successful outcome.

Handling objections is a nuanced and multifaceted skill that requires a combination of empathy, communication, and problem-solving. By embracing objections as opportunities, listening actively, clarifying root causes, responding with value and evidence, turning objections into opportunities, handling objections proactively, seeking win-win solutions, and following up and revisiting as needed, you can effectively navigate objections and build trust with your prospects, ultimately driving meaningful outcomes and fostering long-term success. Embrace this process with an open mind and a spirit of collaboration, and you'll unlock the power of objection handling to achieve your sales goals.

4

Advanced Closing Techniques

Creating a Sense of Urgency

Creating a sense of urgency is a powerful technique used in various contexts, from sales and marketing to project management and personal productivity. It involves leveraging psychological triggers to motivate action and drive results by instilling a feeling of time pressure or scarcity. Let's look into the intricacies of this strategy and explore how it can be applied effectively

1. **Understanding the Psychology**
At the core of creating a sense of urgency lies an understanding of human psychology. Humans are wired to respond to deadlines, scarcity, and the fear of missing out (FOMO). By tapping into these innate cognitive biases, you can motivate people to take action by creating a perceived need to act quickly to avoid missing out on an opportunity or suffering a loss.

2. **Highlighting Limited Availability**
One of the most common ways to create a sense of urgency is by highlighting limited availability.

Whether it's a limited-time offer, a limited quantity of products, or limited slots for an event or service, scarcity creates a sense of urgency by signaling that time is running out to take advantage of the opportunity. By emphasizing the limited availability of your offering, you can encourage people to act quickly to secure their spot or purchase before it's too late.

3. **Setting Clear Deadlines**
Another effective way to create a sense of urgency is by setting clear deadlines. Deadlines create a sense of time pressure and provide a tangible endpoint for action. Whether it's a deadline for a sale, a project milestone, or a promotional offer, setting a deadline communicates to people that they need to act by a certain date or time to avoid missing out on the opportunity. By clearly communicating deadlines and emphasizing the consequences of missing them, you can motivate people to take action promptly.

4. **Emphasizing Consequences of Delay**
Communicating the consequences of delay is a powerful way to create a sense of urgency. Whether it's the risk of missing out on a special offer, the potential for price increases, or the possibility of losing out to competitors, emphasizing the negative consequences of procrastination can motivate people

to act quickly to avoid those outcomes. By highlighting the costs of inaction and the benefits of taking immediate action, you can create a sense of urgency that compels people to act decisively.

5. Using Social Proof and Peer Pressure

Social proof and peer pressure can also be effective tools for creating a sense of urgency. When people see others taking action or making purchases, they're more likely to feel compelled to do the same to avoid missing out or being left behind. By showcasing testimonials, reviews, or examples of others who have benefited from your offering, you can leverage social proof to create a sense of urgency and encourage people to follow suit.

6. Creating FOMO (Fear of Missing Out)

FOMO is a powerful motivator that drives people to take action to avoid feeling left out or regretful. By tapping into people's fear of missing out on a desirable opportunity or experience, you can create a sense of urgency that prompts them to act quickly to seize the moment. Whether it's through exclusive offers, limited-time deals, or VIP access to events, creating a sense of exclusivity and desirability can fuel FOMO and drive action.

7. **Offering Incentives and Rewards**

Incentives and rewards can be effective motivators for creating a sense of urgency. Whether it's offering discounts, bonuses, or special perks for early adopters or fast movers, providing tangible rewards for taking immediate action can incentivize people to act quickly to secure the benefits. By sweetening the deal with incentives and rewards, you can create a sense of urgency that encourages people to act decisively to capitalize on the opportunity.

8. **Maintaining Authenticity and Integrity**

While creating a sense of urgency can be a powerful strategy, it's essential to do so with authenticity and integrity. Misleading or manipulative tactics can backfire and damage trust and credibility in the long run. Instead, focus on communicating honestly and transparently about the urgency of the opportunity and the reasons why people should act quickly. By maintaining authenticity and integrity in your messaging, you can create a genuine sense of urgency that motivates action while building trust and loyalty with your audience.

Creating a sense of urgency is a potent strategy for motivating action and driving results. By leveraging psychological triggers such as scarcity, deadlines, consequences of delay, social proof, and FOMO, you can instill a sense of urgency that compels people to act quickly to seize the opportunity. Embrace this strategy with authenticity and integrity, and you can harness its power to drive meaningful outcomes and foster long-term success.

Using Persuasive Language

Using persuasive language is a skillful art that empowers individuals to influence, inspire, and motivate others to take action or adopt a particular point of view. It involves crafting messages that resonate deeply with the audience, appealing to their emotions, values, and logic to persuade them effectively. Let's embark on an immersive exploration of the intricacies of persuasive language and how it can be wielded to create meaningful impact

1. **Understanding the Power of Words**

Words have the power to shape perceptions, evoke emotions, and drive action. Effective persuasive language begins with an understanding of the nuances of language and the impact that different words and phrases can have on the audience. By choosing words carefully and deliberately, you can convey your message with clarity, conviction, and impact, capturing the attention and imagination of your audience.

2. Appealing to Emotions

Emotions are a potent force in decision-making, and persuasive language leverages this power to influence behavior. By tapping into the audience's emotions—such as joy, fear, anger, or empathy—you can create a strong emotional connection that resonates deeply with them. Whether it's evoking a sense of urgency, stirring up excitement, or appealing to their sense of altruism, appealing to emotions can elicit a visceral response that motivates action.

3. Appealing to Values and Beliefs

People are more likely to be persuaded when the message aligns with their values and beliefs. Persuasive language can leverage this principle by appealing to the audience's core values, ideals, and principles. Whether it's emphasizing the importance of integrity, justice, or freedom, framing your message in terms of values that resonate with the audience can strengthen its persuasive appeal and foster a sense of alignment and resonance.

4. Building Credibility and Trust

Persuasive language is most effective when delivered by a credible and trustworthy source. Building credibility and trust involves demonstrating expertise, authority, and integrity in your communication. Whether it's citing relevant data and evidence, sharing personal anecdotes or testimonials, or showcasing your track record of success, establishing credibility and trustworthiness can enhance the persuasive impact of your message and increase the likelihood of acceptance.

5. Using Social Proof and Authority

Social proof and authority are powerful principles of persuasion that can be leveraged through language. Social proof involves referencing the actions, opinions, or endorsements of others to validate your message and persuade the audience to follow suit. Whether it's citing testimonials, reviews, or endorsements from satisfied customers or influential figures, leveraging social proof can bolster the credibility and persuasiveness of your message. Similarly, appealing to authority—such as citing expert opinions, industry leaders, or credible sources—can lend legitimacy and credibility to your message, increasing its persuasive impact.

6. Framing and Priming

The way a message is framed can significantly influence its persuasive impact. Persuasive language involves framing your message in a way that resonates with the audience and primes them to respond positively. Whether it's framing your argument in terms of benefits versus risks, gains versus losses, or solutions versus problems, choosing the right frame can shape the audience's perception and response. By framing your message strategically, you can increase its persuasive appeal and effectiveness.

7. Using Rhetorical Devices

Rhetorical devices are powerful tools that can enhance the persuasiveness of language. Whether it's using metaphors, analogies, anecdotes, or rhetorical questions, these devices can capture the audience's attention, evoke emotion, and reinforce key points effectively. By incorporating rhetorical devices into your communication, you can add depth, texture, and resonance to your message, making it more memorable and persuasive in the process.

8. Call to Action

Persuasive language culminates in a clear and compelling call to action—a directive that prompts the audience to take a specific course of action. Whether it's urging them to make a purchase, sign up for a newsletter, or support a cause, the call to action serves as the linchpin of persuasive communication. By crafting a clear and compelling call to action that aligns with the audience's interests and motivations, you can convert persuasion into action and drive meaningful outcomes.

Therefore, using persuasive language is a skillful art that combines the science of psychology with the art of communication. By appealing to emotions, values, and beliefs, building credibility and trust, leveraging social proof and authority, framing and priming messages strategically, using rhetorical devices, and culminating in a clear call to action, persuasive language can wield tremendous influence and drive meaningful change. Embrace this art with sincerity, integrity, and empathy, and you'll unlock the power to persuade and inspire others to action.

Trial Closes and Assumptive Closes

Trial closes and assumptive closes are powerful techniques used in sales to gauge a prospect's interest and commitment, as well as to guide them towards making a purchasing decision. These techniques involve subtly testing the waters and assuming the sale to encourage the prospect to move forward with the buying process. Let's explore these techniques in depth

1. **Trial Closes**
   - **Definition**

Trial closes are questions or statements used throughout the sales conversation to gauge the prospect's readiness to make a decision. These questions are designed to elicit feedback and insight into the prospect's level of interest, objections, and concerns.

   - **Purpose**

The purpose of trial closes is to gather information, build understanding, and guide the prospect towards a positive buying decision. By asking trial closes, sales professionals can identify any obstacles or objections early on and address them effectively.

   - **Examples**
     - "How does that sound to you?"
     - "Can you see how this solution could benefit your business?"
     - "Do you have any concerns or questions at this point?"
     - "Would you like to move forward with this option?"

- **Benefits**
  - Provides valuable feedback: Trial closes help sales professionals understand the prospect's mindset and level of interest.
  - Builds understanding: By engaging in a dialogue and asking for feedback, sales professionals can build trust and understanding with the prospect.
  - Guides the conversation: Trial closes help steer the conversation towards a positive outcome by addressing any objections or concerns early on.

2. **Assumptive Closes**
   - **Definition**

Assumptive closes involve assuming the sale and acting as if the prospect has already made the decision to purchase. These techniques are used to subtly guide the prospect towards committing to the purchase without explicitly asking for their decision.

   - **Purpose**

The purpose of assumptive closes is to create a sense of inevitability and encourage the prospect to visualize themselves using the product or service. By assuming the sale, sales professionals can instill confidence and momentum in the buying process.

   - **Examples**
     - "When would you like to get started?"
     - "How many units would you like to order?"

- "Which delivery option works best for you?"
- "Shall we proceed with the paperwork?"

- **Benefits**
  - Creates momentum assumptive closes: keeps the sales process moving forward by encouraging the prospect to take action.
  - Builds confidence: By assuming the sale, sales professionals convey confidence in their product or service, which can help alleviate the prospect's concerns.
  - Encourages visualization: Assumptive closes prompt the prospect to visualize themselves using the product or service, making the decision to purchase feel more natural and inevitable.

3. **Combining Techniques**
   - Synergistic approach: While trial closes and assumptive closes are distinct techniques, they can be used in tandem to maximize their effectiveness. For example, a sales professional might start by asking trial closes to gauge the prospect's level of interest and address any objections, then seamlessly transition to assumptive closes once they sense readiness from the prospect.
   - Flexibility and adaptability: The key to successful implementation is flexibility and adaptability. Sales professionals must be attuned to the prospect's

responses and adjust their approach accordingly, whether it means asking more trial closes to address objections or confidently moving forward with assumptive closes when the prospect shows signs of readiness.

4. Ethical Considerations

- Respectful and transparent: It's essential for sales professionals to use trial closes and assumptive closes ethically and respectfully. These techniques should never be used to pressure or manipulate the prospect into making a decision they're not comfortable with.

- Honesty and integrity: Sales professionals should always maintain honesty and integrity in their interactions with prospects. Assumptive closes should only be used when there is genuine alignment between the prospect's needs and the product or service being offered.

Trial closes and assumptive closes are valuable techniques in the sales process, designed to gauge the prospect's interest, address objections, and guide them towards making a positive buying decision. When used ethically and effectively, these techniques can help sales professionals build understanding, instill confidence, and drive meaningful outcomes. By mastering the art of trial closes and assumptive closes, sales professionals can enhance their effectiveness and achieve greater success in closing deals.

5

Negotiation Strategies

Maximizing Value for Both Parties

Maximizing value for both parties is the cornerstone of successful and sustainable business relationships. It involves creating mutually beneficial outcomes where all parties involved feel that they have gained something of significant worth from the interaction or transaction. Let's look into the maximizing value for both parties across various contexts

1. Understanding Mutual Interests and Objectives
   - Maximizing value begins with a deep understanding of the interests, needs, and objectives of all parties involved. By identifying common ground and shared goals, you can lay the foundation for creating value that benefits everyone.
   - This involves conducting thorough research, asking probing questions, and actively listening to the perspectives of others to gain insight into their priorities and motivations.

2. Collaborative Problem-Solving and Innovation
   - Collaboration is key to maximizing value for both parties. By working together to identify challenges,

explore opportunities, and develop innovative solutions, all parties can contribute their expertise and resources to create value.
   - This collaborative approach fosters creativity, flexibility, and adaptability, allowing for the co-creation of solutions that meet the unique needs and preferences of each party.

3. **Transparent Communication and Information Sharing**
   - Transparency is essential for building trust and maximizing value. Open and honest communication ensures that all parties have access to relevant information and can make informed decisions.
   - By sharing information openly, addressing concerns proactively, and seeking feedback and input from all stakeholders, you can create an atmosphere of trust and collaboration that fosters value creation.

4. **Balancing Short-Term and Long-Term Goals**
   - Maximizing value requires striking a balance between short-term gains and long-term sustainability. While it's important to achieve immediate results, it's equally essential to consider the long-term implications and consequences of decisions.
   - This involves evaluating trade-offs, considering the impact on all stakeholders, and making decisions that optimize value creation over the long term.

5. Flexibility and Adaptability

- Value creation is dynamic and evolving, requiring flexibility and adaptability to changing circumstances and priorities. By remaining open to new ideas, feedback, and opportunities, all parties can adapt their strategies and approaches to maximize value.
- This flexibility allows for agility and responsiveness, enabling parties to pivot when necessary and capitalize on emerging opportunities for value creation.

6. Fair and Equitable Distribution of Benefits

- Maximizing value requires ensuring that benefits are distributed fairly and equitably among all parties involved. This may involve negotiating mutually acceptable terms, setting clear expectations, and honoring commitments.
- By fostering a sense of fairness and equity, you can build trust and goodwill among stakeholders, strengthening relationships and facilitating future collaboration.

7. Continuous Improvement and Evaluation

- Maximizing value is an ongoing process that requires continuous improvement and evaluation. By regularly assessing outcomes, gathering feedback, and identifying areas for improvement, all parties can

refine their strategies and approaches to enhance value creation.
- This commitment to continuous learning and improvement fosters a culture of innovation and excellence, driving sustained value creation over time.

Maximizing value for both parties is about creating win-win outcomes where everyone involved feels that they have gained something meaningful and valuable from the interaction. By understanding mutual interests and objectives, fostering collaboration and innovation, promoting transparent communication and information sharing, balancing short-term and long-term goals, embracing flexibility and adaptability, ensuring fair and equitable distribution of benefits, and committing to continuous improvement and evaluation, all parties can work together to create value that benefits everyone involved. Embrace these principles with sincerity and integrity, and you'll unlock the full potential of value creation in your business relationships.

Win-Win Negotiation Tactics

Win-win negotiation tactics are strategies and techniques used to achieve mutually beneficial outcomes where all parties involved feel satisfied with the result. These tactics prioritize collaboration, problem-solving, and creative thinking to maximize value for both sides of the negotiation. Let's explore these tactics in detail

1. **Focus on Interests, Not Positions**
   - Instead of getting stuck on rigid positions, focus on understanding the underlying interests and motivations of all parties involved.
   - By identifying common interests and shared goals, you can explore creative solutions that address everyone's needs while maximizing value.

2. **Seek to Understand Before Being Understood**
   - Actively listen to the perspectives, concerns, and priorities of the other party before presenting your own.
   - By demonstrating empathy and understanding, you can build understanding and trust, creating a more conducive environment for collaboration and problem-solving.

3. **Generate Options for Mutual Gain**
   - Brainstorm a wide range of potential solutions that could meet the needs and interests of both parties.
   - Encourage creativity and open-mindedness, exploring unconventional ideas and thinking outside the box to uncover mutually beneficial opportunities.

4. Separate People from the Problem

- Keep the focus on the issues at hand and avoid personalizing the negotiation or making it about egos.
- By separating people from the problem, you can maintain a constructive and respectful dialogue that focuses on finding solutions rather than assigning blame.

5. Use Objective Criteria for Evaluation

- Base decisions on objective criteria and standards rather than subjective opinions or preferences.
- By referring to external benchmarks, industry standards, or precedents, you can depersonalize the negotiation process and ensure fairness and equity for all parties involved.

6. Build Trust and Understanding

- Establishing trust and understanding is essential for successful win-win negotiations.
- Be transparent, honest, and reliable in your communications and actions, demonstrating integrity and credibility throughout the negotiation process.

7. Be Willing to Compromise and Flexibility

- Recognize that compromise is often necessary to achieve a mutually beneficial outcome.
- Be flexible and open to adjusting your positions or priorities in exchange for concessions from the other

party, seeking a balance that maximizes value for both sides.

8. Maintain a Positive and Constructive Attitude

- Approach the negotiation with a positive and constructive mindset, focusing on finding solutions rather than dwelling on obstacles or conflicts.
- Cultivate a collaborative spirit and frame the negotiation as an opportunity to create value and build stronger relationships with the other party.

9. Use Active Listening and Effective Communication

- Practice active listening by giving the other party your full attention, paraphrasing their points, and asking clarifying questions to ensure mutual understanding.
- Use clear and concise communication to convey your own interests, priorities, and proposals, avoiding ambiguity or confusion.

10. Prepare Thoroughly and Know Your BATNA (Best Alternative to a Negotiated Agreement)

- Before entering into negotiations, conduct thorough research and preparation to understand the issues at hand and identify potential areas for agreement.
- Know your Best Alternative to a Negotiated Agreement (BATNA) and use it as a benchmark for

evaluating proposed solutions and making strategic decisions during the negotiation.

Therefore, win-win negotiation tactics prioritize collaboration, creativity, and problem-solving to achieve mutually beneficial outcomes where all parties involved feel satisfied with the result. By focusing on interests, seeking to understand before being understood, generating options for mutual gain, separating people from the problem, using objective criteria for evaluation, building trust and understanding, being willing to compromise and flexible, maintaining a positive and constructive attitude, using active listening and effective communication, and preparing thoroughly and knowing your BATNA, you can navigate negotiations successfully and create value for both sides.

6

Overcoming Common Challenges

Dealing with Rejection

Dealing with rejection in the context of closing deals can be particularly challenging, given the high stakes and competitive nature of sales environments. However, mastering the art of coping with rejection is essential for sales professionals to maintain motivation, resilience, and effectiveness in their roles. Let's explore strategies for handling rejection in the sales process

1. **Develop a Resilient Mindset**
   - Cultivate a resilient mindset that allows you to bounce back from rejection quickly and effectively.
   - Recognize that rejection is a normal part of the sales process and doesn't define your worth as a salesperson.

2. **Embrace a Growth Mindset**
   - Adopt a growth mindset that focuses on learning and improvement rather than fixed outcomes.
   - See rejection as an opportunity for growth and self-reflection, rather than a personal failure.

3. **Analyze and Learn from Rejections**
   - Instead of dwelling on the disappointment of rejection, analyze the reasons behind it and look for areas where you can improve.
   - Seek feedback from prospects or colleagues to gain insight into what went wrong and how you can adjust your approach in the future.

4. **Stay Positive and Maintain Confidence**
   - Maintain a positive attitude and belief in your abilities, even in the face of rejection.
   - Remind yourself of past successes and strengths to boost your confidence and motivation.

5. **Focus on the Process, Not Just the Outcome**
   - Shift your focus from solely closing deals to the process of building relationships, solving problems, and adding value to your prospects.
   - By focusing on the process, you can derive satisfaction from the effort and progress you make, regardless of the outcome.

6. **Practice Persistence and Resilience**
   - Understand that closing deals often requires persistence and resilience in the face of repeated rejections.
   - Stay committed to your goals and keep pushing forward, even when faced with setbacks.

7. Develop Coping Strategies

- Identify coping strategies that help you deal with the emotional impact of rejection, such as exercise, meditation, or talking to a supportive colleague.
- Find healthy ways to manage stress and recharge your energy so that you can approach each new opportunity with a fresh perspective.

8. Stay Organized and Proactive

- Stay organized in your sales activities and maintain a proactive approach to prospecting and follow-up.
- By staying on top of your pipeline and taking proactive steps to engage with prospects, you can increase your chances of success and minimize the impact of rejection.

9. Seek Support and Guidance

- Lean on your colleagues, mentors, or sales managers for support and guidance during challenging times.
- Share your experiences and learn from others who have faced similar challenges in their sales careers.

10. Celebrate Small Wins and Milestones

- Celebrate your successes, no matter how small, to boost morale and maintain motivation.

- Recognize and reward your efforts, whether it's reaching out to a certain number of prospects or securing a meeting with a key decision-maker.

Dealing with rejection in the context of closing deals requires a combination of resilience, positivity, and self-reflection. By developing a resilient mindset, embracing a growth mindset, analyzing and learning from rejections, maintaining confidence, focusing on the process, practicing persistence and resilience, developing coping strategies, staying organized and proactive, seeking support and guidance, and celebrating small wins and milestones, sales professionals can navigate rejection with grace and emerge stronger and more effective in their roles. Remember that each rejection brings you one step closer to success, and use it as an opportunity for growth and self-improvement in your sales journey.

Handling Difficult Clients

Handling difficult clients is an inevitable aspect of business, whether you're in sales, customer service, consulting, or any other client-facing role. While challenging, effectively managing difficult clients is crucial for maintaining positive relationships, preserving your reputation, and ultimately achieving success. Here's an in-depth exploration of strategies for handling difficult clients

1. Stay Calm and Professional
- Maintain your composure and professionalism, regardless of the client's behavior or demeanor.
- Avoid reacting emotionally or defensively, as this can escalate tensions and exacerbate the situation.

2. Listen Actively and Empathize
- Practice active listening by giving the client your full attention and demonstrating empathy for their concerns.
- Validate their feelings and show understanding of their perspective, even if you don't agree with it.

3. Set Clear Boundaries and Expectations
- Clearly define boundaries and expectations for the client relationship from the outset.
- Communicate these boundaries respectfully but firmly, and enforce them consistently to maintain respect and professionalism.

4. Communicate Effectively
- Use clear and concise communication to convey information, address concerns, and manage expectations.

- Be proactive in providing updates and addressing issues promptly to prevent misunderstandings or frustrations from escalating.

5. Focus on Solutions, Not Problems
- Approach difficult situations with a problem-solving mindset, focusing on finding solutions rather than dwelling on the problems.
- Collaborate with the client to identify actionable steps and mutually agreeable resolutions to address their concerns.

6. Manage Expectations Realistically
- Set realistic expectations for what you can deliver and when, based on your capabilities and resources.
- Be transparent about any limitations or constraints that may impact the client's expectations, and work together to find alternatives or compromises.

7. Establish Trust and Understanding
- Build trust and understanding with the client through consistent communication, reliability, and follow-through on commitments.
- Demonstrate integrity and honesty in your interactions, even when delivering difficult news or feedback.

8. Stay Solution-Oriented

- Keep the focus on finding solutions that meet the client's needs and goals, rather than dwelling on past grievances or assigning blame.
- Approach challenges with a collaborative mindset, seeking input and feedback from the client to inform decision-making and problem-solving.

9. Know When to Escalate

- Recognize when a situation requires escalation to higher levels of authority or involvement, such as a manager or supervisor.
- Be prepared to escalate tactfully and diplomatically, providing clear documentation and rationale for your decision.

10. Learn and Grow from Challenges

- View difficult client interactions as opportunities for growth and learning.
- Reflect on the experience afterward to identify lessons learned and areas for improvement in your client management approach.

11. Maintain Self-Care

- Prioritize self-care and well-being to prevent burnout and maintain resilience in the face of challenging situations.

- Take breaks when needed, seek support from colleagues or mentors, and practice stress-reduction techniques to manage the emotional toll of dealing with difficult clients.

12. **Know When to Walk Away**
- In some cases, despite your best efforts, it may be necessary to walk away from a client relationship that is consistently problematic or incompatible.
- Assess the costs and benefits of continuing the relationship, and be prepared to make the difficult decision to disengage if necessary for your well-being and the well-being of your business.

In essence, handling difficult clients requires a combination of patience, empathy, communication skills, and problem-solving abilities. By staying calm and professional, actively listening and empathizing, setting clear boundaries and expectations, communicating effectively, focusing on solutions, managing expectations realistically, establishing trust and understanding, staying solution-oriented, knowing when to escalate, learning and growing from challenges, maintaining self-care, and knowing when to walk away, you can effectively navigate challenging client interactions and maintain positive relationships that contribute to your long-term success.

7
Closing the Deal

Asking for the Sale

Asking for the sale is an important step in the process of closing business deals. It's the moment when a sales professional must confidently and effectively communicate the value proposition of their product or service, address any remaining objections or concerns, and invite the prospect to make a purchasing decision. Mastering the art of asking for the sale requires finesse, persuasion, and strategic communication. Let's look deeply into this topic to explore key strategies and best practices for asking for the sale

1. Timing is Key
   - Choose the right moment to ask for the sale, ideally after you've thoroughly qualified the prospect, addressed their concerns, and built understanding and trust.
   - Look for buying signals such as positive body language, verbal affirmations, or questions about pricing or next steps to gauge readiness.

2. Be Confident and Assertive

- Approach the ask with confidence and assertiveness, demonstrating belief in the value and benefits of your product or service.
- Use assertive language and tone to convey your conviction and enthusiasm, while also respecting the prospect's autonomy and decision-making process.

3. Clearly Articulate the Value Proposition

- Clearly communicate the unique value proposition of your offering, emphasizing the benefits and outcomes that the prospect stands to gain.
- Highlight how your product or service addresses the prospect's specific needs, pain points, or challenges better than alternative solutions.

4. Address Remaining Objections

- Anticipate and address any remaining objections or concerns the prospect may have before asking for the sale.
- Use active listening to understand the prospect's hesitations and objections, and respond with empathy and clarity to alleviate their concerns.

5. Create a Sense of Urgency

- Create a sense of urgency by highlighting time-sensitive incentives, limited-time offers, or impending price increases.

- Emphasize the benefits of acting now rather than later, such as immediate access to solutions, cost savings, or competitive advantages.

6. Offer Assurances and Guarantees

- Offer assurances and guarantees to reduce the prospect's perceived risk and increase their confidence in making the purchase.
- Provide warranties, satisfaction guarantees, or money-back guarantees to demonstrate your commitment to customer satisfaction and confidence in your offering.

7. Provide Clear Next Steps

- Provide clear and concise instructions on what the prospect needs to do next to complete the purchase.
- Guide the prospect through the buying process step-by-step, outlining any necessary paperwork, contracts, or payment arrangements.

8. Use Trial Closes

- Use trial closes throughout the sales conversation to gauge the prospect's readiness to move forward.
- Ask questions such as "If we were able to address your concerns, would you be ready to move forward today?" to test the waters and identify any remaining barriers to closing.

9. **Assume the Sale**
   - Approach the ask with an assumptive mindset, assuming that the prospect is ready to buy and simply needs guidance to complete the process.
   - Use language that assumes the sale, such as "When would you like to get started?" rather than "Would you like to proceed?" to instill confidence and momentum.

10. **Follow Up and Persist**
    - If the prospect hesitates or expresses uncertainty, follow up with additional information, testimonials, or references to reinforce the value proposition.
    - Persist in your efforts to close the sale, while also respecting the prospect's decision-making process and timeline.

11. **Stay Professional and Respectful**
    - Maintain a professional demeanor and respectful attitude throughout the ask, regardless of the prospect's response.
    - Accept rejection gracefully and thank the prospect for their time and consideration, leaving the door open for future opportunities or referrals.

12. **Learn and Iterate**
   - After each sales interaction, reflect on what worked well and areas for improvement in your approach to asking for the sale.
   - Continuously learn from your experiences, gather feedback from colleagues or mentors, and iterate on your strategies to become more effective in closing business deals.

Asking for the sale is a crucial step in the sales process that requires confidence, persuasion, and strategic communication. By timing you ask appropriately, being confident and assertive, clearly articulating the value proposition, addressing objections, creating a sense of urgency, offering assurances, providing clear next steps, using trial closes, assuming the sale, following up and persisting, staying professional and respectful, and learning and iterating, sales professionals can effectively close business deals and drive revenue growth for their organizations.

Closing Techniques for Different Scenarios

Closing techniques are essential tools in a salesperson's arsenal for effectively sealing the deal and converting prospects into customers. Different scenarios call for different closing techniques, depending on factors such as the prospect's needs, objections, and buying signals. Let's explore a variety of closing techniques tailored to different scenarios in the sales process

1. The Assumptive Close

- **Scenario** The prospect has expressed interest and seems ready to move forward.
- **Technique** Assume the sale by using language that implies the prospect has already decided to buy, such as "When would you like to get started?" or "Which option works best for you?"

2. The Direct Close

- **Scenario**

The prospect is straightforward and prefers a no-nonsense approach.

- **Technique**

Simply ask for the sale directly, using clear and concise language, such as "Are you ready to move forward with this?" or "Can we finalize the details today?"

3. The Alternative Close

- **Scenario**

The prospect is considering multiple options or solutions.

- **Technique**

Present two or more options and ask the prospect to choose between them, such as "Would you prefer option A or option B?" or "Which package best meets your needs?"

4. The Summary Close
- **Scenario**

The prospect has expressed interest but needs a recap of the benefits and value proposition.

- **Technique**

Summarize the key benefits and features of your offering, then ask for confirmation, such as "Based on what we've discussed, are you ready to move forward?"

5. The Urgency Close
- **Scenario**

The prospect is interested but hesitant to commit.

- **Technique**

Create a sense of urgency by highlighting time-sensitive incentives or limited-time offers, such as "This special pricing is only available until the end of the month" or "We have limited availability, so I recommend securing your spot today."

6. The Trial Close
- **Scenario**

The prospect needs reassurance or confirmation before making a decision.

- **Technique**

Ask trial closing questions throughout the sales conversation to gauge the prospect's readiness, such as "If we were able to address your concerns, would you be ready to move forward?"

7. The Fear-of-Missing-Out (FOMO) Close
- **Scenario**

The prospect is interested but needs an extra push to commit.

- **Technique**

Highlight the potential consequences of not taking action, such as missing out on a limited-time offer, losing competitive advantage, or falling behind competitors.

8. The Now-or-Never Close
- **Scenario**

The prospect is on the fence and needs a decisive push.

- **Technique**

Present a compelling reason to act now, such as a special promotion, limited availability, or impending price increase, and ask for an immediate commitment.

9. The Question Close
- **Scenario**

The prospect is undecided and needs guidance to make a decision.

- **Technique**

Ask closing questions that prompt the prospect to consider the benefits of your offering and envision the positive outcomes of moving forward, such as "How would this solution help you achieve your goals?" or "Can you see yourself benefiting from our product/service?"

10. The Silence Close
- **Scenario**

The prospect seems interested but is hesitant to make a decision.

- **Technique**

After presenting your offer, remain silent and allow the prospect time to process the information and respond. Often, the discomfort of silence prompts the prospect to make a decision or provide feedback.

11. The Puppy Dog Close
- **Scenario**

The prospect is hesitant to commit due to concerns or objections.

- **Technique**
Offer a trial or demonstration of your product or service, allowing the prospect to experience its benefits firsthand. This reduces perceived risk and increases the likelihood of a positive buying decision.

12. **The Referral Close**
   - **Scenario** The prospect is interested but needs reassurance from others.
   - **Technique** Offer references, testimonials, or case studies from satisfied customers who have had success with your offering. Social proof can help alleviate doubts and build trust.

Mastering a variety of closing techniques is essential for sales professionals to effectively navigate different scenarios and successfully close deals. By understanding the prospect's needs, objections, and buying signals, and selecting the appropriate closing technique for each situation, sales professionals can increase their chances of sealing the deal and driving revenue for their organizations. Practice, adaptability, and empathy are key to becoming proficient in closing deals across diverse sales scenarios.

8
Follow-Up and Customer Retention

Post-Sale Relationship Building

Post-sale relationship building is a critical aspect of business that often gets overlooked in the pursuit of closing deals. However, nurturing and maintaining relationships with customers after the sale is essential for fostering loyalty, driving repeat business, and generating referrals. It involves ongoing engagement, support, and communication to ensure that customers are satisfied, valued, and loyal to your brand. Let's explore this topic in depth:

1. **Express Gratitude and Appreciation**
   - Start by expressing sincere gratitude and appreciation to customers for their business and trust in your products or services.
   - Send personalized thank-you notes, emails, or gestures to show customers that their support is valued and appreciated.

2. **Provide Ongoing Support and Assistance**
   - Offer ongoing support and assistance to customers to address any questions, concerns, or issues they may have after the sale.

- Make yourself accessible through multiple channels, such as phone, email, chat, or social media, to ensure that customers can reach out to you easily when needed.

3. Deliver on Promises and Commitments
- Continuously deliver on the promises and commitments you made during the sales process to maintain trust and credibility with customers.
- Fulfill orders promptly, provide timely updates on delivery status, and honor any warranties or guarantees associated with your products or services.

4. Personalize Communication and Engagement
- Personalize your communication and engagement with customers to make them feel valued and understood.
- Use customer data and insights to tailor your messages, offers, and recommendations to each customer's preferences and interests.

5. Solicit Feedback and Act on It
- Actively seek feedback from customers on their experiences with your products or services, and use this feedback to make improvements.
- Regularly solicit input through surveys, reviews, or direct conversations, and demonstrate that you are listening and taking action based on their feedback.

6. Offer Exclusive Benefits and Rewards

- Provide exclusive benefits and rewards to loyal customers as a token of appreciation for their continued support and loyalty.

- Offer discounts, special offers, or access to VIP programs that incentivize repeat business and encourage customers to remain engaged with your brand.

7. Educate and Empower Customers

- Educate and empower customers with resources, tutorials, or training materials that help them get the most out of your products or services.

- Provide tips, best practices, and use cases to help customers maximize their value and achieve their goals with your offerings.

8. Keep Customers Informed and Engaged

- Keep customers informed and engaged with regular updates, newsletters, or communications that provide valuable information, insights, or industry news.

- Stay top-of-mind by sharing relevant content, tips, or updates that demonstrate your expertise and thought leadership in your field.

9. Celebrate Milestones and Achievements

- Celebrate milestones and achievements with customers to reinforce the positive relationship and show appreciation for their loyalty.
- Recognize anniversaries, birthdays, or other significant events with personalized messages, gifts, or special offers.

10. Foster a Community and Sense of Belonging

- Foster a sense of community and belonging among your customers by creating opportunities for them to connect with each other.
- Host events, forums, or online communities where customers can share experiences, ask questions, and interact with your brand and other customers.

11. Anticipate and Proactively Address Needs

- Anticipate the evolving needs and preferences of your customers and proactively offer solutions or recommendations to meet those needs.
- Stay informed about industry trends, customer feedback, and market developments to stay ahead of the curve and remain relevant to your customers.

12. Measure and Track Customer Satisfaction

- Measure and track customer satisfaction through metrics such as Net Promoter Score (NPS), customer satisfaction surveys, or retention rates.

- Use this data to assess the effectiveness of your post-sale relationship building efforts and identify areas for improvement.

Post-sale relationship building is a vital component of customer success and business growth. By expressing gratitude and appreciation, providing ongoing support and assistance, delivering on promises, personalizing communication, soliciting feedback, offering exclusive benefits, educating and empowering customers, keeping customers informed and engaged, celebrating milestones, fostering community, anticipating needs, and measuring satisfaction, businesses can nurture strong and enduring relationships with customers that lead to long-term loyalty, advocacy, and success.

Ensuring Customer Satisfaction

Ensuring customer satisfaction is a cornerstone of success for any business, as it directly impacts customer loyalty, retention, and advocacy. A satisfied customer is not only likely to return for repeat business but also to refer others, contributing to the growth and success of the organization. Let's explore in detail the strategies and practices for ensuring customer satisfaction across various aspects of business:

1. **Understanding Customer Needs and Expectations**
   - Begin by gaining a deep understanding of your customers' needs, preferences, and expectations.
   - Conduct market research, analyze customer feedback, and gather insights to identify what matters most to your target audience.

2. **Providing High-Quality Products or Services**
   - Deliver products or services that meet or exceed customer expectations in terms of quality, reliability, and performance.
   - Invest in product development, innovation, and quality assurance processes to ensure consistent delivery of high-quality offerings.

3. **Offering Exceptional Customer Services**
   - Provide prompt, courteous, and personalized customer service at every touchpoint, including pre-sale inquiries, sales interactions, and post-sale support.
   - Train and empower frontline staff to address customer inquiries, resolve issues, and exceed expectations through proactive and empathetic communication.

4. **Building Trust and Credibility**
   - Foster trust and credibility with your customers by delivering on your promises, honoring commitments,

and demonstrating integrity and transparency in all interactions.

- Establish a reputation for reliability, professionalism, and ethical business practices that instills confidence and loyalty among customers.

5. Creating Positive Customer Experiences

- Focus on delivering memorable and positive experiences throughout the customer journey, from initial contact to post-purchase follow-up.

- Personalize interactions, anticipate customer needs, and go above and beyond to delight customers at every opportunity.

6. Soliciting and Acting on Feedback

- Actively seek feedback from customers through surveys, reviews, and direct communication channels.

- Use customer feedback to identify areas for improvement, address pain points, and enhance the overall customer experience.

7. Providing Ongoing Support and Assistance

- Offer ongoing support and assistance to customers after the sale, such as technical support, training resources, or product updates.

- Demonstrate a commitment to long-term customer success by providing resources and assistance to help customers derive maximum value from your products or services.

8. Maintaining Accessibility and Convenience
- Make it easy for customers to do business with you by providing multiple channels for communication, purchasing, and support.
- Ensure that your website, mobile app, and other digital platforms are user-friendly, intuitive, and accessible to customers of all backgrounds and abilities.

9. Rewarding Loyalty and Advocacy
- Recognize and reward loyal customers through loyalty programs, exclusive offers, or personalized incentives.
- Encourage satisfied customers to become advocates for your brand by sharing their positive experiences with others through referrals, testimonials, or online reviews.

10. Continuous Improvement and Innovation
- Commit to continuous improvement and innovation to stay ahead of evolving customer needs and expectations.
- Monitor market trends, gather customer insights, and adapt your products, services, and processes to remain relevant and competitive in the marketplace.

11. Measuring and Monitoring Customer Satisfaction

- Implement metrics and key performance indicators (KPIs) to measure customer satisfaction, such as Net Promoter Score (NPS), customer satisfaction surveys, or customer retention rates.

- Regularly monitor and analyze customer feedback and performance data to identify trends, track progress, and make informed decisions to improve customer satisfaction.

12. Cultivating a Customer-Centric Culture

- Foster a customer-centric culture within your organization by emphasizing the importance of customer satisfaction at all levels.

- Empower employees to prioritize customer needs and make decisions that prioritize long-term customer relationships over short-term gains.

Ensuring customer satisfaction requires a thorough approach that encompasses product quality, customer service, customer experiences, feedback management, ongoing support, accessibility, loyalty rewards, continuous improvement, measurement, and a customer-centric culture. By prioritizing customer satisfaction and making it a central focus of your business strategy, you can build strong relationships, foster customer loyalty, and drive sustainable growth and success for your organization.

9
Measuring Success

Key Performance Indicators

Key Performance Indicators (KPIs) are essential metrics used by sales organizations to measure the effectiveness and success of their efforts in closing deals. By tracking and analyzing these KPIs, sales teams can gain valuable insights into their performance, identify areas for improvement, and make data-driven decisions to optimize their sales processes. Let's explore the key performance indicators relevant to closing deals in detail

1. Win Rate

- Win rate measures the percentage of opportunities or leads that result in a successful sale.
- Calculated by dividing the number of won deals by the total number of opportunities or leads and multiplying by 100.
- A high win rate indicates that the sales team is effectively converting leads into customers, while a low win rate may suggest issues with qualification, negotiation, or value proposition.

2. Conversion Rate

- Conversion rate measures the percentage of prospects or leads that take a desired action, such as making a purchase or signing a contract.
- Calculated by dividing the number of conversions by the total number of leads or opportunities and multiplying by 100.
- Provides insight into the efficiency of the sales funnel and the effectiveness of lead nurturing and qualification efforts.

3. Average Sales Cycle Length

- Average sales cycle length measures the average time it takes to convert a lead into a customer, from initial contact to deal closure.
- Calculated by summing the total duration of all sales cycles and dividing by the number of deals closed.
- Helps identify bottlenecks, inefficiencies, or delays in the sales process that may be impacting closing rates.

4. Average Deal Size

- Average deal size measures the average monetary value of closed deals.
- Calculated by dividing the total value of closed deals by the number of deals closed.

- Provides insights into the value proposition of your products or services and the effectiveness of upselling or cross-selling efforts.

5. Opportunity-to-Win Ratio
- Opportunity-to-win ratio measures the percentage of qualified opportunities that result in a successful sale.
- Calculated by dividing the number of won deals by the total number of qualified opportunities and multiplying by 100.
- Helps assess the quality of lead qualification and the likelihood of success for future opportunities.

6. Pipeline Velocity
- Pipeline velocity measures the speed at which opportunities move through the sales pipeline, from initial contact to deal closure.
- Calculated by dividing the total value of closed deals by the average length of the sales cycle.
- Indicates the efficiency and effectiveness of the sales process in converting leads into customers.

7. Customer Acquisition Cost (CAC)
- Customer acquisition cost measures the average cost of acquiring a new customer, including sales and marketing expenses.

- Calculated by dividing the total sales and marketing expenses by the number of new customers acquired.
- Helps assess the efficiency and ROI of sales and marketing efforts in acquiring new business.

8. Customer Lifetime Value (CLV)

- Customer lifetime value measures the total value of a customer over the entire duration of their relationship with the company.
- Calculated by multiplying the average annual revenue per customer by the average customer lifespan.
- Provides insights into the long-term value and profitability of acquired customers, guiding decisions around customer retention and loyalty.

9. Sales Velocity

- Sales velocity measures the rate at which revenue is generated through the sales pipeline.
- Calculated by multiplying the number of opportunities by the average deal size and win rate, and dividing by the average length of the sales cycle.
- Helps forecast future revenue and identify opportunities for improving sales performance and efficiency.

10. **Lead Response Time**

- Lead response time measures the time it takes for sales representatives to respond to incoming leads or inquiries.

- Calculated as the average time elapsed between lead submission and initial contact by a sales representative.

- Faster response times are associated with higher conversion rates and improved customer satisfaction.

11. **Churn Rate**

- Churn rate measures the percentage of customers who discontinue their relationship with the company over a specific period.

- Calculated by dividing the number of lost customers by the total number of customers and multiplying by 100.

- High churn rates may indicate issues with customer satisfaction, product quality, or ongoing support.

12. **Sales Forecast Accuracy**

- Sales forecast accuracy measures the accuracy of sales predictions and projections made by the sales team.

- Calculated by comparing forecasted sales figures to actual sales results over a given period.

- Helps improve sales planning, resource allocation, and decision-making based on more reliable and accurate forecasts.

Tracking and analyzing key performance indicators related to closing deals is essential for optimizing sales performance, driving revenue growth, and achieving business success. By monitoring metrics such as win rate, conversion rate, average sales cycle length, average deal size, opportunity-to-win ratio, pipeline velocity, customer acquisition cost, customer lifetime value, sales velocity, lead response time, churn rate, and sales forecast accuracy, sales organizations can gain valuable insights into their performance, identify areas for improvement, and make informed decisions to enhance their closing rates and overall sales effectiveness.

Analyzing and Improving Closing Rates

Analyzing and improving closing rates is crucial for sales professionals and organizations seeking to maximize their effectiveness and achieve greater success in closing deals. Closing rates, also known as conversion rates, measure the percentage of leads or prospects that ultimately result in a successful sale. By analyzing closing rates and implementing strategies to improve them, sales teams can increase revenue, optimize resource allocation, and drive business growth. Let's delve deeply into this topic to explore key strategies for analyzing and improving closing rates

1. **Define Key Metrics and KPIs**
   - Start by defining the key metrics and key performance indicators (KPIs) that are relevant to your sales process and objectives.
   - This may include metrics such as lead conversion rate, opportunity-to-win ratio, average sales cycle length, and win rate by sales representative.

2. **Collect and Analyze Data**
   - Gather data on your sales activities, leads, opportunities, and outcomes using a reliable CRM (Customer Relationship Management) system or sales analytics tools.
   - Analyze this data to identify trends, patterns, and areas of improvement in your closing rates and sales process.

3. **Segment Leads and Opportunities**
   - Segment your leads and opportunities based on various criteria such as industry, company size, geographic location, or stage in the sales funnel.

- Analyze closing rates for different segments to identify which types of leads or opportunities are most likely to convert into customers.

4. Identify Bottlenecks and Obstacles
- Identify bottlenecks and obstacles in your sales process that may be contributing to low closing rates.
- Common bottlenecks may include lengthy sales cycles, lack of qualified leads, ineffective communication, or objections from prospects.

5. Address Objections and Overcome Barriers
- Develop strategies and tactics for addressing common objections and overcoming barriers to closing deals.
- Provide sales training and resources to equip your sales team with the skills and techniques they need to handle objections effectively and move prospects towards a positive buying decision.

6. Improve Lead Qualification
- Refine your lead qualification process to ensure that you are focusing your time and resources on leads that are most likely to convert into customers.
- Use lead scoring criteria, qualification questions, and behavior tracking to identify high-quality leads and prioritize follow-up activities.

7. Streamline the Sales Process

- Streamline your sales process to reduce friction and complexity, making it easier for prospects to move through the buying journey.
- Identify and eliminate unnecessary steps or inefficiencies in the sales process that may be hindering your ability to close deals.

8. Enhance Sales Collateral and Presentations

- Invest in creating high-quality sales collateral, presentations, and proposals that effectively communicate the value proposition of your products or services.
- Tailor your sales materials to address the specific needs, pain points, and objections of your target audience, increasing the likelihood of closing deals.

9. Improve Sales Team Training and Development

- Provide ongoing training and development opportunities for your sales team to enhance their skills, knowledge, and confidence.
- Focus on areas such as negotiation tactics, objection handling, closing techniques, and product knowledge to empower your sales team to close deals more effectively.

10. Implement Sales Enablement Tools and Technology

- Leverage sales enablement tools and technology to streamline your sales process, automate repetitive tasks, and provide valuable insights and analytics.
- Use tools such as CRM software, sales engagement platforms, and predictive analytics to optimize your sales efforts and improve closing rates.

11. **Encourage Collaboration and Knowledge Sharing**
- Foster a culture of collaboration and knowledge sharing within your sales team, encouraging team members to share best practices, insights, and success stories.
- Create opportunities for peer-to-peer learning, mentorship, and collaboration to help your sales team continuously improve and learn from each other.

12. **Monitor and Measure Progress**
- Continuously monitor and measure your progress towards improving closing rates, using your defined metrics and KPIs as benchmarks.
- Track changes in closing rates over time, and evaluate the effectiveness of the strategies and initiatives you have implemented to identify areas for further improvement.

Analyzing and improving closing rates requires a systematic and data-driven approach that encompasses various aspects of the sales process, from lead generation to deal closure. By defining key metrics and KPIs, collecting and analyzing data, segmenting leads and opportunities, identifying bottlenecks and obstacles, addressing objections, improving lead qualification, streamlining the sales process, enhancing sales collateral and presentations, investing in sales team training and development, implementing sales enablement tools and technology, encouraging collaboration and knowledge sharing, and monitoring and measuring progress, sales professionals and organizations can optimize their closing rates and achieve greater success in closing deals.

10
Case Studies and Examples

Real-Life Scenarios and Solutions

Real-life scenarios in closing deals often present various challenges and opportunities that sales professionals must navigate to achieve successful outcomes. Let's explore some common scenarios encountered in the sales process, along with effective solutions for addressing them

1. **Dealing with Price Objections**
- **Scenario**
A prospect expresses hesitation or objections regarding the price of your product or service.
- **Solution**
Instead of immediately offering discounts, focus on demonstrating the value and ROI of your offering. Provide examples of how your solution can help the prospect save money, increase efficiency, or achieve their goals. Offer flexible pricing options or payment plans to accommodate budget constraints while still delivering value.

2. Handling Competitor Comparison
- **Scenario**

The prospect compares your offering to a competitor's solution and expresses uncertainty about the differences.

- **Solution**

Differentiate your product or service by highlighting unique features, benefits, or advantages that set it apart from competitors. Provide case studies, testimonials, or references from satisfied customers to reinforce your value proposition. Focus on building trust and credibility by demonstrating your expertise and understanding of the prospect's specific needs and challenges.

3. Overcoming Indecision or Procrastination
- **Scenario**

The prospect shows interest but hesitates to make a decision or delays the buying process.

- **Solution**

Address any concerns or objections the prospect may have and provide additional information or resources to help them make an informed decision. Offer incentives or limited-time promotions to create a sense of urgency and encourage action. Follow up regularly and stay engaged with the prospect to keep the momentum going and move them towards a positive buying decision.

4. Managing Stakeholder Buy-In
- **Scenario**

The prospect is interested in your offering, but key stakeholders within their organization need to be convinced.

- **Solution**

Engage with all relevant stakeholders and decision-makers to understand their priorities, concerns, and requirements. Tailor your messaging and presentations to address the specific needs and interests of each stakeholder. Provide evidence, data, or case studies that demonstrate the value and benefits of your solution in addressing their challenges and achieving their objectives.

5. Navigating Complex Buying Processes
- **Scenario**

The sales process involves multiple decision-makers, departments, or layers of approval, leading to delays or complications.

- **Solution**

Map out the buying process and identify all stakeholders involved, along with their roles and responsibilities. Build relationships and understanding with each stakeholder and engage them throughout the process. Provide clear and concise information to facilitate decision-making and address any concerns or objections promptly. Use collaboration tools or CRM software to streamline communication and coordination among team members and stakeholders.

6. Closing Large or Enterprise Deals
- **Scenario**

Closing deals with large enterprises or complex organizations requires navigating lengthy sales cycles and multiple stakeholders.

- **Solution**

Develop a strategic account management approach that focuses on building long-term relationships and delivering value at every stage of the sales process. Engage with key decision-makers and influencers across different departments and levels of the organization. Customize your solutions to address the unique needs and challenges of the enterprise, and demonstrate scalability, reliability, and ROI to justify the investment.

7. Handling Rejection or Lost Opportunities
- **Scenario**

Despite your best efforts, a prospect decides not to move forward with your offering.

- **Solution**

Accept rejection gracefully and use it as an opportunity to learn and improve. Seek feedback from the prospect to understand their reasons for not proceeding and identify areas for enhancement. Stay positive and resilient, and continue to nurture relationships with prospects who may reconsider in the future or refer others to your business. Focus on generating new opportunities and moving forward rather than dwelling on lost deals.

8. Negotiating Terms and Contracts
- **Scenario**

Negotiating terms, pricing, or contract details with the prospect involves compromises and concessions.
- **Solution**

Prepare thoroughly for negotiations by understanding the prospect's needs, priorities, and constraints. Set clear objectives and boundaries for the negotiation and prioritize win-win outcomes that benefit both parties. Focus on finding common ground and creative solutions that address the prospect's concerns while protecting your interests. Maintain open communication and flexibility throughout the negotiation process to build trust and goodwill.

Real-life scenarios in closing deals require sales professionals to be adaptable, strategic, and customer-focused. By understanding the prospect's needs, addressing objections, building trust and credibility, and providing value at every stage of the sales process, sales professionals can overcome challenges, seize opportunities, and achieve successful outcomes in closing deals. Effective communication, negotiation skills, and relationship-building are essential for navigating complex sales scenarios and driving business growth.

Conclusion

Closing Deals is about more than just sealing the immediate transaction—it's about fostering long-term relationships, driving mutual success, and creating value that endures over time. By celebrating achievements, reflecting on lessons learned, reaffirming commitments, setting expectations, encouraging communication, promoting additional value, expressing confidence and optimism, reinforcing partnerships, inviting collaboration, and expressing gratitude and appreciation, sales professionals can lay the foundation for sustained success and growth in closing deals.

About the Author

The author of the book "Mastering the Art of Closing Deals" is a professional with years of experience in the industry. The author has worked with various companies from startups to huge establishments, honing her skills in negotiation, persuasion and deal-making. Through her book, she shares practical strategies, real life scenarios and great tips to help sales professionals master the art of closing deals effectively. Her insight is pinpoint on years of hands-on experience and a deep understanding of human psychology and buying behavior. "Mastering the Art of Closing Deals" is widely regarded as a must read for anyone looking to excel in sales and achieve greater success in closing deals.

www.ingramcontent.com/pod-product-compliance
Lightning Source LLC
Chambersburg PA
CBHW050314230526
45471CB00005B/2182